Alexander Wegner
Am Blauen Camp 11G
21335 Lüneburg
Deutschland
E-Mail: creative@wegner-designs.de

Printed in Great Britain
by Amazon

34892486R00070